AUSTRALIAN
SHEPHERD PUPPY TRAINING

AUSTRALIAN SHEPHERD PUPPY TRAINING

© Copyright 2021 - All rights reserved.

The content contained within this book may not be reproduced, duplicated or transmitted without direct written permission from the author or the publisher.

Under no circumstances will any blame or legal responsibility be held against the publisher, or author, for any damages, reparation, or monetary loss due to the information contained within this book. Either directly or indirectly.

Legal Notice:

This book is copyright protected. This book is only for personal use. You cannot amend, distribute, sell, use, quote or paraphrase any part, or the content within this book, without the consent of the author or publisher.

Disclaimer Notice:

Please note the information contained within this document is for educational and entertainment purposes only. All effort has been executed to present accurate, up to date, and reliable, complete information. No warranties of any kind are declared or implied. Readers acknowledge that the author is not engaging in the rendering of legal, financial, medical or professional advice. The content within this book has been derived from various sources. Please consult a licensed professional before attempting any techniques outlined in this book. By reading this document, the reader agrees that under no circumstances is the author responsible for any losses, direct or indirect, which are incurred as a result of the use of information contained within this document, including, but not limited to, errors, omissions, or inaccuracies.

AUSTRALIAN SHEPHERD PUPPY TRAINING

Table Of Contents

INTRODUCTION 8
    THE HISTORY AND BACKGROUND OF THE AUSTRALIAN SHEPHERD 9
    BEHAVIORAL CHARACTERS 10
    INTELLIGENCE 10
    A WORKING ANIMAL 10
    LEADERSHIP QUALITIES 11
    GREAT COMPANION 11
    PHYSICAL DESCRIPTION 12

CHAPTER 1: CHARACTERISTICS OF THE AUSTRALIAN SHEPHERD 14

CHAPTER 2: WHY TRAINING IS IMPORTANT IN A PUPPY AUSSIE 20
    TRAINING WILL BUILD A TRUSTING BOND BETWEEN YOU AND YOUR PUP .. 20
    TRAINING CAN PREVENT BAD BEHAVIORS FROM OCCURRING LATER IN LIFE 21
    TRAINING CAN HELP YOU TO ENFORCE THE RULES YOU SET FOR YOUR PUP 21
    TRAINING YOUR AUSSIE WILL HELP HIM TO BE MORE CONFIDENT AND MAKE YOUR PUP A BETTER COMPANION 21
    TRAINING IS A GREAT WAY TO BOND WITH YOUR NEW PUP 22

CHAPTER 3: WHY IT IS IMPORTANT TO LET HIM VENT PHYSICALLY AND MENTALLY 24

CHAPTER 4: HOW TO PREPARE FOR THE PUPPY ARRIVAL . 30
    BUYING DOG SUPPLIES 30
    RELATIONSHIP 34
    PUPPY PROOFING YOUR HOME 34
    PUT UP ANY HAZARDOUS ITEMS 35
    PUPPY'S EYE VIEW 35
    PUT KNICK-KNACKS UP HIGH 35
    CLOSE OFF ACCESS TO STANDING WATER 36
    TIE UP THOSE ELECTRICAL CORDS AND DRAPERY CORDS 36
    KEEP GARBAGE OUT OF REACH OR IN A PUPPY PROOF CONTAINER 37
    BLOCK OFF STAIRS 37

KEEP DOORS CLOSED 38
CHECK THE OUTDOORS 38
LOOK AT YOUR PLANTS 38
THE RIGHT SPOT 39

CHAPTER 5: FIRST DAYS WITH A PUPPY AUSSIE 40

A LOT OF ACCIDENTS 40
SOME FRUSTRATIONS 41
SOME LEEWAY 41
A CLEAN SLATE 41
LACK OF SLEEP 42
A LOT OF SUPPORT 42
MANY PICTURES INVOLVED 42
A STRONG BOND 43
A HAPPY HOME 43

CHAPTER 6: DISCIPLINE AND DEALING WITH UNWANTED BEHAVIORS 44

HOW TO DEAL WITH A PROBLEM BEHAVIOR BEFORE IT BECOMES A HABIT 44
HELPFUL TIPS 46

CHAPTER 7: START TRAINING 50

START TRAINING YOUR AUSSIE EARLY 50
WHEN TO START TRAINING 50
POSITIVE REINFORCEMENT AND NOT PUNISHMENT 51
CONSISTENCY IS THE KEY 52
SECRETS OF POTTY TRAINING 53
SECRETS TO LEASH TRAINING YOUR AUSSIE 55

CHAPTER 8: PHYSICAL AND MENTAL EXERCISE 58

GOLDEN RULES TO DEVELOP A STRONG BOND WITH YOUR AUSSIE 59

CHAPTER 9: DOG LANGUAGE 64

ALL THE WAGGING AND BARKING 66
WHAT THE WAG MEANS 66
WHAT THE BARK MEANS 69

CHAPTER 10: HAND CUES 82

THE USEFULNESS OF HAND CUES 82

"Sit" Hand Cue 82
"Stay" Hand Cue 83
"Down" Hand Cue 84
"Leave it" Hand Cue 85
"Quiet" Hand Cue 86
"Come" Hand Cue 87
"Good Boy" Hand Cue 88

CHAPTER 11: THE BASIC COMMANDS 90

Sit 90
Come 91
Down 91
Stay 92
Fetch 92
Drop It 93
Leave It 93

CHAPTER 12: POSITIVE REINFORCEMENT 96

Treats 98
Types of Treats 100
How and When to Treat 102
Bribery vs. Reward Dog Treating 104

CHAPTER 13: NEGATIVE REINFORCEMENT 106

CHAPTER 14: TAKING CARE OF YOUR PUPPY 114

Find a Good Vet 114
Food 115
Feeding Schedule 116
Obedience Training 116
Bathroom Training 117
Be Social 118
Signs of Illness 118
Spaying and Neutering 119

CHAPTER 15: SOCIALIZING WITH PEOPLE AND ANIMALS .. 120

CONCLUSION 124

Introduction

If you have decided to raise an Australian Shepherd, it's important to understand the breed's personality and to plan the raising program with full focus on the behavior of the dog. Australian Shepherds sometimes display extreme changes or ups and downs in their behavior while growing, and hence preceding understanding of such temperament fluctuations can help the owners during training and grooming.

The History and Background of the Australian Shepherd

Although the Australian Shepherd is named as such, it is not considered Australian at all. This breed is known to have developed most probably in the Pyrenees Mountains amidst the land of France and Spain. In addition to this, this breed is believed to have refined in the western US to work on ranches as a herding dog in the 1840s around the period of the Gold Rush. In truth, the confusion about Aussie's origin is just one of the numerous misconceptions about this well-skilled and useful herding dog.

The Australian Shepherd's primary forefathers were most probably Spanish dogs which accompanied the shepherds of the Merino sheep that were sold or traded to both Australia and America as well as the Basque shepherds in the preceding days of the colonies. It is believed that at some point in time, this breed possibly crossed with the Collie stock. The Australian Shepherd has had several names before, including Spanish Shepherd, Pastor Dog, Bobtail, Blue Heeler, California Shepherd, and the New American Shepherd. This breed is known to possess a great number of talents, such as herding, guarding, retrieving, narcotics detection, watchdog, performing tricks, police work, search and rescue, competitive obedience, and agility.

Behavioral Characters

The Australian Shepherd dog is an intellectual and versatile animal, mainly a working dog with great herding and caretaker attributes. He is an excellent friend. He can be easily trained and can execute assigned tasks with elegance and great passion. He is aloof among outsiders but does not show nervousness. Some of the other qualities of this breed are aggressive nature and commanding helper. They have less tolerance if people or other creatures irritate them.

Intelligence

The intelligence of the Australian Shepherd dog can be inferred by their independent thinking process and problem-solving techniques. They are very optimistic in every situation they encounter. This is an essential attribute in Australian Shepherds who work excellently with stock, and it transfers to other roles of life also. Australian Shepherd owners should attentively teach their pets their limitations before they misunderstood their opportunities.

A Working Animal

Aussies require mental motivation at the same level as physical exercise. There should be a healthy equilibrium related to this trait; otherwise, it can cause problems. For this dog, problem-solving is not only a personality attribute but a stimulus. They adore challenges, and they love the accomplishment after solving a problem. Most of the dog owners offer necessary volumes of physical exercises to their Aussies but fail to give enough mental motivation and hence affecting the growth of the dog.

Leadership Qualities

The skill to confidently boss livestock everywhere is a quality that has been flagged by breeders for a long time now. Australian Shepherds are natural leaders; they enjoy keeping things in order; and they are capable of having an influence. Hence, it can be said that if control and leadership become weak, then Aussies are skilled enough to perform under the leadership role.

Great Companion

Aussies are very good friends, they desire to know what you want from them, and they stay enthusiastic about obeying when they understand the expectations. While working as livestock dogs, they willingly alter strategies and study the needs of their trainer. They feel anxiety if they are left with objectives and attempt to perform activities that might not be ideal. They are determined and rebound willingly from uneasiness or injury that may occur on the job. Aussies can endure extreme conditions. If you find your Aussie worried about pain, then it is a matter of seriousness, and it is necessary to examine the problem immediately. They are protective by nature.

Physical Description

Lifespan

An Australian Shepherd will normally live between 10 and 13 years old.

However, it is not uncommon for an Australian Shepherd to live as old as 15, providing that it does not develop any serious health issues.

Height and Weight

A fully-grown Australian Shepherd will normally be between 18 and 23 inches (45.75 to 58.5cm) tall at the shoulder. A healthy adult Australian Shepherd will normally weigh between 40 and 65 pounds (18 to 30kg)—dependent upon their size.

Breed Characteristics

The following unit will give you a simplistic overview of the characteristics of an Australian Shepherd.

Our rating system is from 1 to 10—with 1 being the lowest score and 10 being the highest.

- Adaptability: 6/10
- Friendliness: 8/10
- Health: 4/10
- Ease of Grooming: 1/10
- Amount of Shedding: 6/10
- Trainability: 10/10
- Intelligence: 10/10
- Exercise Needed: 10/10
- Playfulness: 10/10
- Family Friendliness: 10/10

Color and Appearance

Australian Shepherds come in a wide variety of colors, including black, blue merle, red and red merle. Dogs can also be solid or have white markings, as well as tan points, depending on the genes. The coat is of a medium length and can either be straight to slightly wavy in style. It is generally short around the head, ears, and the front of the legs.

CHAPTER 1:

Characteristics of the Australian Shepherd

Did you know that, according to the World Canine Association (FCI), there are officially more than 350 canine breeds recognized today?

Your Australian Shepherd dog is only one of many different breeds. Naturally, many have things in common. After all, every dog is a descendent, one way or another, from his remote ancestor, the wolf. You can see it more in some breeds than in others.

Here, I would like to give you a brief summary of this fascinating breed so that you know what you are letting yourself in when you choose an Australian Shepherd.

The Australian Shepherd is one of the most popular dog breeds in Germany, not only because of his beautiful appearance but also because of his highly intelligent, friendly, and loving character.

Let us start by dispelling one of the biggest misunderstandings about this dog; the Australian Shepherd does not originate from Australia. The word "Australian" does not refer to his place of origin but to the fact that, at the beginning of the 19th Century, he was used in the United States of America, the real origin of this dog, to guard "Australian Sheep."

The character of the "Aussie," as he is known to enthusiasts, is that he is a typical working dog. He is intelligent, persevering, and even-tempered. He is more sensitive and cautious towards people he does not know, but he builds close ties with his family. Because of his background as a working dog, he is able to concentrate on his work for extended periods and is able to make his own decisions, if necessary. This means that if he gets very bored, he makes his own decision on how to occupy himself, which does not always match the expectations of his owner.

For this reason, I do not recommend the Australian Shepherd for beginners. He is challenging and requires loving consistency in his upbringing and a lot of exercise in his everyday life. A beginner would be overwhelmed very quickly. However, if you are a very active and nature-loving person, the Australian Shepherd is the right partner for you.

His long-life expectancy of 13-15 years makes him a late developer and not really mature until he is 2-3 years old. For you, this means that in the first few years, he will not only require a lot of your energy, expertise, and patience, but you will also need to cater to and commit to the typical characteristics of this kind of dog.

It will not be enough only to have gentle walks with your little friend. On the contrary, he will need a lot of variety and needs to be given tasks challenging to him. Three long walks at minimum, with short play breaks, such as fetching exercises, should be planned into your daily routine. Jogging, hiking, and biking are possible pursuits you can carry out with your dog, as well as almost any kind of dog sport. It will be easy to summon his enthusiasm for most kinds of activities.

Even though he has the need for lots of exercises, you should not forget that your Australian Shepherd also needs to have breaks to settle him down again. It is important that you teach him that in his first year. An Aussie that has never learned to settle will become an adrenalin junkie, always on the move and looking for his next adventure.

Australian Shepherds are regarded as intelligent creatures. This can be helpful during his training as he learns extremely quickly to recognize patterns and has a lot of fun learning and practicing. However, his intelligence means that he does not only learn positive things very quickly but also recognizes the mistakes you make in his training and is able to exploit them. For this reason, too, it is useful to have experience in dog training before you choose an Australian Shepherd.

Because Australian Shepherds are affectionate and very friendly creatures, who love being petted, your new friend would make a perfect family pet. You should pay particular attention to small children because your Australian Shepherd may tend to be over-protective and to round them up as if they were his own herd.

His protective nature can also turn very quickly into a hunting instinct. This does not have to be the case, but you need to know that it is a possibility. If this could be a problem for you, perhaps the Australian Shepherd is not the right dog for you.

On average, an Australian Shepherd reaches a size of 18 to 23 inches (shoulder height) and a weight of 37 to 60 pounds. His fur is mid-length, and he has two basic colors: Black and red. Additionally recognized colors are blue merle (background color black with the typical lighter patches) and red merle (background color red with the typical lighter patches), whereas there are a lot of different manifestations.

Now you can see what a wonderful breed you have chosen! On the following pages, you can find a short portrait of the breed, according to the FCI standard.

These pages are not enough to give you a full picture of this magnificent animal. However, I hope I have been able to draw you a picture of what it is like to own an Australian Shepherd. Of course, there are always dogs that do not conform to this description, and some have much stronger or weaker characteristics, but I hope that you are able to recognize your Australian Shepherd in this description.

Short breed portrait according to the FCI:

Country of Origin	USA
Character	Intelligent, strong herding and guarding instincts, loyal companion, the stamina to work all day, good-natured, seldom quarrelsome
Height at withers	Males: 51 - 58 cm Females: 46 - 53 cm
Weight	Males: 19 - 28 kg Females: 15 - 22 kg
Eyes	Brown, blue, amber, or any variation or combination thereof, almond-shaped

Ears	Triangular, set high on the head
Fur and Fur Color	Short, smooth, with undercoat Blue merle, black, red merle, red—all with or without white markings and/or tan markings.
FCI-Classification	Group 1: Sheepdogs and Cattle dogs Section 1: Sheepdogs
Usage	Farm and ranch shepherd dog

CHAPTER 2:

Why Training Is Important in a Puppy Aussie

Training your pup is the most important step in making a happy and healthy dog. Training teaches your pup rules and boundaries, and this builds trust between you and your dog. It also helps to teach manners, like waiting at doors or not jumping up on people. Similarly, it training pups early in life can help avoid behavior problems down the line. Here are several reasons why you should train your Australian Shepherd:

Training Will Build a Trusting Bond Between You and Your Pup

A pup that is well trained knows the rules and realizes that you are in charge, and this will build trust between you. This is important because it helps your pup to feel safe around you, which greatly reduces anxiety. Pups that do not have very strong bonds with their owners are often more hyperactive or anxious when left alone.

Training Can Prevent Bad Behaviors From Occurring Later in Life

Teaching rules early in life can help prevent behavior issues from developing over time. For example, if your pup is accustomed to waiting at doors for permission to enter rooms or go outdoors, he is less likely to jump up on people or slip by you outdoors later on in life.

Training Can Help You to Enforce the Rules You Set for Your Pup

Well-trained Aussie Shepherds know the rules and realize that you are in charge. They know that if they misbehave, they will be corrected. For example, a well-trained dog knows that when outdoors, he must sit-stay before crossing an invisible boundary. So, he will automatically sit when approaching boundaries that he knows (like those of your yard).

Training Your Aussie Will Help Him to Be More Confident and Make Your Pup a Better Companion

Well-trained pups feel safe and are secure in their world. They are more relaxed, and this helps them to be better companions to you.

They also tend to be calmer because they know that behaviors will probably turn out OK if they follow the rules that you set for them.

Training Is a Great Way to Bond With Your New Pup

Training with your new pup will allow you to form a more secure bond early in life. Pups that participate in training with their owners are more likely to spend time with you, and this can be wonderful when you are trying to work as a team.

Puppies respond best to positive reinforcement, so remember that treats and rewards will be most helpful. Be sure not to get frustrated if training does not go well at first, as it takes time for pups to learn how humans communicate.

It is also important that you do not go overboard when training your pup.

Training is also necessary because it helps to strengthen your bond with your dog early on in life—and this will have an impact even later on down the line. So, to be successful with training your pup, it is imperative to start early. Start teaching basic obedience commands when your Aussie is young and then continue to add new stuff as he grows.

Training will help you to raise a happy, confident, well-adjusted dog that can adjust easily to any environment.

CHAPTER 3:

Why It Is Important to Let Him Vent Physically and Mentally

One of the major reasons why dog owners should not keep their puppies in a small confined space is that their puppy doesn't have an adequate outlet for his pent-up energy. A puppy with a lot of pent-up energy will not be happy and will likely act out in destructive ways, which can often lead to behavioral issues that are difficult to break. In addition, you may find yourself frustrated or anxious as your pup seemingly does nothing all day long.

Here are several reasons:

1. A puppy with pent-up energy can be destructive.
2. Your puppy will develop behavioral issues that will make it difficult for him to be placed in an adoptive home or to be adopted into the family. Most often, dogs are returned to a shelter due to behavioral issues, and the shelter has to euthanize them.

3. It is cruel to keep your puppy confined just because you don't know how to vent his energy or have a fear of heights/elevators/anything that might frighten your pup, so you keep him on the ground floor in a small area for his entire life.
4. Contrary to popular belief, placing your pup in a small confined area does not teach him where his boundaries are. In fact, keeping your puppy in a small confined space teaches him that you are the source for all of his needs. This will make him dependent and insecure. Confinement also inhibits the development of both physical and mental growth.
5. Finally, there is no reason you need to keep your dog in a small confined space until he has learned basic obedience commands such as sit, down, and stay (unless you are actively working on these exercises).

The truth is that confinement is not necessary in most cases. The best way to prevent behavioral issues is to allow your puppy the chance to physically and mentally vent on a regular basis. This does not mean you have to spend hours a day exercising your puppy. Five minutes at a time 2 or 3 times a day (depending on the age of your puppy) is plenty of exercise. If you want, you can do this before work, as part of breakfast and dinner time, before bedtime, or anytime during the day when you are home. You can take him for a walk or run around for five minutes in the backyard and play fetch with him or engage in other physical activities (ball toss, tug-of-war, etc.).

If you don't want to do this yourself, you can hire a dog walker or someone else in the family who is willing to exercise your puppy on a regular basis.

The bottom line is that you should not keep your puppy confined to a small area for long periods of time (i.e., most of the day). If you do, there is a good chance that he will develop behavioral issues such as excessive barking or chewing, separation anxiety, predatory behavior, and so on.

I cannot stress enough how important it is for all dogs to learn how to vent their energy and have opportunities to release their pent-up frustration. It is tantamount to weight control for humans; just as you must exercise and eat right to maintain your good health, your dog must be allowed the same opportunity.

A lot of people are afraid to allow their puppy opportunities to vent because they don't know how they will react. I assure you that if you expose your puppy to venting experiences on a regular basis from an early age, he will have no problem accepting a wide variance of stimuli. In fact, he may even enjoy them.

There are two key questions you need to ask yourself in order to determine whether or not your pup needs opportunities for venting:

1. How well does my puppy react to close interactions with people?
2. How well does my puppy react to sudden movements or sounds?

If your puppy has demonstrated that he is uncomfortable with close interactions with people or is fearful of sudden movements, then you should begin venting opportunities immediately. Start by taking him on walks and allowing him to sniff all of the smells along the way, including other dogs, people, cars, and so on. Then take him for a jog where he can burn off some energy. If you don't have access to a fenced-in yard where your pup can play fetch, you can buy a ball that bounces off walls, such as the Kong Squeezz Ball, so that he can exercise indoors.

Your puppy should also be allowed opportunities to run as fast as he wants to on a leash. Remember, just because he doesn't seem like he is getting enough exercise, that doesn't mean that is the case. Although some puppies are very energetic, others are not, so you will have to monitor your own pup carefully and let him guide you.

Of course, each person's experience with this will vary. Many puppies from single dog families or those raised in very quiet homes do not require additional opportunities for venting until they reach adolescence or adulthood.

If you have a multi-dog household or your puppy has demonstrated that he is comfortable with a wide array of stimuli, then you can begin venting opportunities as early as 8 to 12 weeks of age.

Of course, there are exceptions to every rule, so if your puppy doesn't appear to need additional opportunities for venting or has demonstrated that he is comfortable with close interactions or sudden movements, you will need to wait until your puppy reaches adolescence or adulthood before you expose him to various stimuli.

It should also be noted that although the majority of dogs do not require daily walks and runs, it does not mean that they don't enjoy them. Dogs have a lot of energy, and they like to burn it off as often as possible. Whether you choose to allow your puppy opportunities for venting or not, he will still need to be exercised on a regular basis. Some people choose to exercise their pups on a daily basis, while others do so every other day or once or twice per week.

If you choose not to expose your puppy to various stimuli on a regular basis, then you will have to compensate by playing tug-of-war with him in the backyard, running around the living room furniture, throwing his toys back and forth, and playing fetch with him so many times that he is too tired to chew up any items that are not his own.

CHAPTER 4:

How to Prepare for the Puppy Arrival

Getting a puppy is always exciting, and part of that excitement comes from everything you need to purchase for your puppy. While every dog owner is different, there are some common supplies that you should purchase for your Australian Shepherd.

It is important to note that the list of supplies you need for a puppy is pretty basic, and you do not need to purchase everything that is recommended by your pet store. Here we will look at the supplies that are absolute necessities and supplies that are optional. We will also look at ways for you to puppy-proof your home.

Buying Dog Supplies

You don't need a lot of things when you are getting started with your puppy. However, it is important to have your supplies before you bring your puppy home. You must have bowls and puppy food ready before you need them, for example. And it is best not to take your puppy shopping with you before he has his vaccinations.

Supplies that you should have for your puppy are:

Feeding Bowls

Make sure that you have a water and food bowl that your puppy can reach easily. Stainless steel bowls are best. They are more durable, they don't break, they are easy to clean, and they don't allow bacteria to grow. Ceramic bowls are also a good choice, provided they are dishwasher safe. However, if they crack, they can allow bacteria to grow. Plastic bowls are not a good choice. Some dogs can be allergic to plastic, and it will cause a reaction on their nose and muzzle. Scratches on the plastic can also harbor bacteria.

Collar

Purchase a flat collar for your Australian Shepherd puppy that will fit him when he comes home. Puppies grow quickly, so most people purchase a nylon collar for a young puppy instead of purchasing expensive collars that will quickly be outgrown. The general rule is to get a collar that will allow you to put two fingers between the collar and your puppy's throat. That should be comfortable for your puppy to wear.

Leash

A 6-foot flat leash is a good choice for a puppy the size of an Australian Shepherd. You can easily get a leash that matches your puppy's collar. Remember to use a leash that is comfortable in your hand as well as sturdy. Although you won't need it right away, you may want to purchase a 20-foot lead for teaching the "come" command later.

Dog Grooming Items

Australian Shepherds do not require a lot of grooming, but they do need to be brushed regularly. While you do not need every type of dog grooming item out there, it is important to have the minimum items for grooming.

Crate

A crate is a good idea for an Australian Shepherd. While some people do not like them, they are very helpful during housetraining. Besides, it will keep your puppy safe when you can't watch him or are out. Crates are not puppy jails. They are a den for dogs, and most puppies and dogs enjoy spending time in them. Dogs are naturally denning creatures, and in the wild, it was a place for them to retreat to sleep, relax, and have their pups in without the fear of predators. The same is true for your puppy; crates provide a good place to relax and sleep.

Toys

Toys are not optional for puppies and dogs. They are a necessity. When your puppy begins chewing on something, you can reach for a toy and distract your Australian Shepherd from chewing. If you have ever had a puppy chew your woodwork or furniture, you know that it is much better to spend a little money on toys to entertain your puppy than spend a lot of money repairing your living room.

Cleaning Supplies

While not a puppy item, cleaning supplies are necessary for bringing a puppy home. Purchase carpet and floor cleaners with enzymes to prevent further soiling. Make sure to use non-toxic cleaners because your dog or puppy will be very close to the flooring, not to mention it could lick your feet, the flooring, or even its paws. Cleaners with labels such as "all-natural" or "eco-friendly" should be okay (not contain solvents, alcohols, or others), but always double-check before purchasing. Also, stock up on paper towels. You will need them.

Dog Bed

Finally, purchase a dog bed or a crate bed for your puppy. Even if you allow your puppy up on the furniture, it is good to have something for him to lay on in the crate.

A soft faux sheepskin mat is popular with many owners and their dogs. Or, you can use some comfy blankets.

Relationship

You should include quality time with your Aussie in your schedule every day. An Australian Shepherd thrives when he can spend time with his owner. This does not have to be time-consuming but can be as simple as sitting down and petting him while you watch TV.

Take the time to make your Australian Shepherd happy, and you will find he is a wonderful companion you love spending time with.

Puppy Proofing Your Home

Puppy proofing your home is a good way to ensure you and your Australian Shepherd get off to a good start together. Otherwise, he could cheerfully destroy your house while he investigates it. Puppies, especially Australian Shepherds, are smart little guys, and they are very curious about everything.

It is important to puppy-proof your home to prevent that destruction before your Australian Shepherd comes home. To properly puppy-proof your home, follow the tips below.

Put up Any Hazardous Items

Pick up and lock away any items that can be hazardous to your Australian Shepherd. These include:

1. Household cleaners
2. Vitamins
3. Medication
4. Vehicle fluids, such as antifreeze
5. Salts for ice or water softener
6. Pool / lawn chemicals
7. Tobacco products

Puppy's Eye View

Take the time to crawl around your home before your puppy arrives and then once or twice a week. Look at things from your puppy's vantage point. Pick up small clips, tags, paper, anything that can be a choking hazard for the puppy.

Also, keep clothes picked up. It can be surprising, but some articles of clothing, such as socks, can pose a choking hazard for your Australian Shepherd.

Put Knick-Knacks up High

While you may love having your ornaments on tables and shelves, look at what your Australian Shepherd can reach. If he can get it, move it up out of reach. Wagging tails have a way of knocking things off balance.

Puppies also like to explore by putting things in their mouths. Putting your objects away will prevent the item from being broken and your puppy from getting hurt. It does not have to be permanent but only until your Australian Shepherd learns what he is and is not allowed to touch.

Close Off Access to Standing Water

Close toilet seat lids, drain tubs and sinks and block off any access to a pool if you have one. Standing water can be very tempting for an Australian Shepherd. However, young puppies cannot swim, and falling into the water could lead to drowning.

Tie Up Those Electrical Cords and Drapery Cords

Electrical cords are always very tempting for a puppy and are often chewed. Always tape your cords out of reach of your puppy. Also, look for cords that dangle from furniture as they may knock a clampdown on themselves while playing with a cord. Do not forget about the computer and phone cords. Make sure they are tucked away if possible.

In addition to electrical cords, pull up the drape or blind cords. These can lead to strangulation if the puppy gets caught in them.

Keep Garbage Out of Reach or in a Puppy Proof Container

Another tempting item for puppies is the garbage can. Always keep it put up where the puppy can't get at it, and make sure you empty it every night, especially if your puppy isn't sleeping in his crate. Bathroom garbage cans are a great source of interest and contain a good deal of hazards like discarded razors, q-tips, cotton balls, etc. It is ideal to have trash cans with a lid to minimize the chance of investigation by curious puppies.

Block Off Stairs

Even if you allow your Australian Shepherd upstairs with you, block off the stairs at both the top and the bottom. Puppies do not have a lot of coordination, and taking stairs can be difficult for them. It is quite common for a puppy to fall downstairs. To prevent this, keep the stairs blocked and off-limits.

Keep Doors Closed

Any door or window leading to the outside should be kept closed if the puppy can access it. An open door can be irresistible for a puppy.

Check the Outdoors

Also, to puppy-proof your house, make sure that you check the outdoors. Look for openings in the fence and items that can be hazardous to your Australian Shepherd puppy. If there are any drain pipes, pools, or other items in your yard, they can present a risk. If you find anything, pick up all the hazardous items and fence or block off the rest, such as the pool or drainpipes. The goal is to make the outdoors as safe as indoors.

Look at Your Plants

Finally, look at the plants that you have in your home and garden. Many plants are poisonous to dogs, so avoid having them in your home. If you do have them, make sure they are in areas where your puppy cannot reach them.

In the end, puppy-proofing is simply keeping your house neat and tidy—and taking a few precautions. Everyone in the home should work with you to keep the space clean, and you should constantly reassess if your house is still safe for your puppy.

The Right Spot

"Outside" is probably not a specific enough spot for you for his evacuation. You probably don't want him to think of your whole yard as his toilet, especially if you have kids. So be consistent and take him to the exact spot you want him to use. Once there, give him a specific one-word command. He'll quickly learn to head to the right spot at this command.

Choose another simple command to use when you want him to relieve himself. This will help him remember what to do, and you'll find it helpful when you are out and about and need to instruct him to use a new place away from home—so pick a word you won't be embarrassed to use in public! "Do your business" or "get busy" are good choices.

CHAPTER 5:

First Days With a Puppy Aussie

You've probably heard that Aussie puppies are rather high maintenance, but you won't believe the lengths we've gone to! We only have two rules in our house—no wet noses and no muddy paws. It's been a long week of adjustments, but now things seem to be running smoothly—until one of us forgets and the other gets peeved over it. What should we do?

Puppy love is inevitable, but with responsibilities come sacrifices! These are just some of the trials and tribulations we have had to deal with in our first week as new puppy owners. Read on for more information on what you can expect when adopting a younger pup to your home. Here are what you can expect to happen:

A Lot of Accidents

When your Aussie pup is first introduced to the house, it's common for him or her to have accidents. A puppy can't hold it forever, and they usually get distracted by important things like balls and toys. It's best just to expect this and be prepared for it—after all, you want to get your puppy onto a schedule as soon as possible!

Some Frustrations

Many new puppy owners have told us their dogs will whine or bark when they have to go to the bathroom. This is a phase they'll grow out of, but in the meantime, you might need a little reassurance that everything's okay. If your pup does this, try rubbing their noses or giving them treats, as well as praising them after you take them out.

Some Leeway

It's important to remember that your puppy can't be perfect all the time—he or she is learning! If they make a mistake now and then, remind yourself that you're raising them for years to come, and it's all part of the process.

A Clean Slate

We have to clean up after our Aussie pup every day, but this is really a small price to pay for such a loving companion! If we tried to use the same mentality as when raising human children, we'd never get anything done! Remember to congratulate yourself for what's not broken and focus on your successes rather than failures.

Lack of Sleep

Puppies are naturally nocturnal creatures, but you'll likely still want to sleep at a reasonable hour. If your pup whines or barks in the night, try setting up a routine and keeping them occupied until they fall asleep. Then tiptoe into your bedroom. If your puppy is an early riser, try to keep them distracted during the day.

A Lot of Support

Remember that there's a whole community around you who are just as excited about your puppy as you are! They can be a great help in easing some of the struggles you experience with your little Aussie pup, and they should be able to offer unique perspectives on the challenges that arise in raising a new dog.

Many Pictures Involved

If you love taking pictures, you're going to have a lot of opportunities to do so with your Aussie! They're happy and smiley no matter what they're doing—and with good reason! You'll want to preserve these memories, as they'll be some of your best.

A Strong Bond

With patience and hard work comes an immensely rewarding relationship between you and your pup—one that can last a lifetime. If you already have children, consider getting an Australian Shepherd as a family pet; the breed is known for watching over children while at home as well as being family-oriented in general.

A Happy Home

By the end of the week, you'll have a new member of your household who will make you smile every time he or she comes bounding in from outside—even if it's covered in mud! With your pup by your side, there's nothing to worry about—except what kind of mischief he or she will get into next!

CHAPTER 6:

Discipline and Dealing with Unwanted Behaviors

How to Deal With a Problem Behavior Before It Becomes a Habit

Everyone likes his or her own space to feel comfortable, familiar, and safe, and your dog is no different. A proper living area is a key factor to avoiding all kinds of potential problems. Think of all the things your puppy will encounter during his life with humans, such as appliances and mechanical noises that are not common in nature and can be frightening to your dog. It is essential to use treats, toys, and praise to assist you and your dog while in the midst of training and socializing.

Dogs are social creatures, and it is essential to communicate with them. Communication is always the key to behavior reinforcement. Regularly rewarding calm behavior and showing that you control their favorite objects and toys, acts as a pathway to thwarting problems that can surface later.

Keep your Mini Aussie's world happy. Make sure he or she is getting a proper amount of exercise and that he is being challenged mentally. Make sure he is receiving enough time in the company of other dogs and other people. Keep a close eye on his diet, offering him good, healthy, dog-appropriate foods. Avoid excessive helpings when treating him.

It is important that you are a strong leader. Dogs are pack animals, and your dog needs to know that you are the leader. Do not let situations become questionable scenarios in which your dog is uncertain about who is in charge. Your puppy will feel confident and strong if he works for his rewards and knows that he or she has a strong and confident leader to follow. Let your dog show you good behavior before you provide him with rewards.

Your dog's first step towards overcoming the challenges in life is in understanding what motivates his behavior. Some behaviors your dog will exhibit are instinctual. Chewing, barking, digging, jumping, chasing and leash pulling are things that all dogs do because it is in their genetic makeup. These natural behaviors differ from the ones we have inadvertently trained into the domestic canine.

Behaviors, such as nudging our hands to be petted or barking for attention, are accidentally reinforced by people and are not innate and should never be rewarded.

What motivates your dog to do what he does or does not do? You may wonder why he does not come when you call him while he is playing with other dogs. Simply, this may be because coming to you is far less exciting than scrapping with the same species. When calling your dog, you can change this behavior by offering him a highly coveted treat and, after treating him, allow him to continue playing for a while.

Start this training aspect slowly and at short distances from where he is playing. Gradually increase the distances and distractions when you beckon your dog. After he is regularly coming to you, then begin to treat him less frequently and supplement it with verbal or physical praise.

Helpful Tips

Here are some helpful tips to use when trying to help your Miniature Australian Shepherd through challenging behavior.

- Are you accidentally rewarding bad behavior? Remember that your dog may see any response from you as a reward. You can ignore the bad behavior if you are patient enough, or you can give your puppy the equivalent of a human time out for a few minutes. Make sure the time-out environment is a calm, quiet and safe place, but a very dull place that is not his crate.

- Think about the quality of his diet and health. Is your dog getting enough playtime, mental and physical exercise, and sleep? Is this a medical problem? Do not ignore the range of possibilities that could be eliciting your dog's challenging behavior. An unseen physical or mental deformity or ailment could be the cause of a chronic negative behavior.
- Be sure and practice replacement behavior. Reward him with something that is much more appealing than the perceived reward that he is getting when he is acting in an undesirable manner. It is important to reward his good behavior before he misbehaves. If done consistently and correctly, this will reinforce good behaviors and reduce poor behaviors.
- For example, in the hopes of receiving love, your dog is repeatedly nudging your hand; instead, teach him to sit by only giving him love after he sits, and never if he nudges you. If you command, "Sit," and he complies, and then you pat him on the head or speak nicely to him, or both, your dog will associate compliance with sitting with nice things.
- If your pooch nudges you and you turn away and never acknowledge him, he will understand that behavior is not associated with nice things. In a scenario where your dog is continually nudging you for attention, catch him before he comes running into your room and

begins nudging you. When you see him approaching, immediately say, "Sit," to stop him in his tracks.

- While practicing the replacement behavior, be sure you reward the right response and ignore the mistakes. Remember, any response to the wrong action could be mistaken as a reward by your dog, so try to remain neutral when you ignore him, which includes visual, touch, and verbal acknowledgment. Be sure to offer your dog a greater reward for the correct action than the joy he is getting from doing the wrong action.

- Your dog's bad behavior may be caused by something that makes him fearful. If you decipher this as the problem, then change his mind about what he perceives as frightening. Pair the scary thing with something he loves. For example, your dog has a problem with the local skateboarder. Pair the skateboarder's visit with a delicious treat and lots of attention. He will soon look forward to the daily arrival of the skateboarder.

- Always remain patient with your dog and do not force changes. Work gradually and slowly. Forcing behavioral changes on your dog may lead to worsening unwanted behavior. Training requires that you work as hard as your dog and maybe harder because you have to hone your observational skills, intuition, timing, patience, laughter, and understanding of your dog's body language and demeanor.

CHAPTER 7:

Start Training

Start Training Your Aussie Early

Who's a good boy (or girl)? Your dog is, of course. Now you are about to learn the secrets to training your dog to do what you want. When you follow these steps, you can raise your Aussie, a dog who is obedient and easy to discipline. He will do what you exactly want when you want, while loving every minute of it.

When to Start Training

Start training the minute your new Aussie enters your life. It is ideal to start at eight weeks when you wean a puppy from his mother. But you can really start at any age. While it is somewhat true that older dogs are a bit harder to train, this does not mean that they are impossible. Dog treats and lots of touch praising with repetition speak volumes to all ages in a dog's lifespan. You can accomplish a lot with an older dog.

The secret to training is to be a dominant figure that your dog respects. You must establish dominance by consistently disciplining your Australian Shepherd and rigorously rewarding him when he does what you want. Don't tolerate behaviors you don't like and always reward the ones you do like. Your dog will understand that you are a master who is responsible for his care, not a pushover who feeds him and does his bidding.

The other secret is to be reliably consistent always. Never give up. Every day is a new day to enforce your rules and teach new tricks or commands. Work on training every day to really cement it into his wonderful, happy, hard noggin. Expect your dog to obey, reward him for it, and take mild disciplinary action when he does not.

Positive Reinforcement and Not Punishment

Never, ever punish your Australian Shepherd for not doing what you want. Instead, teach him not to engage in bad behaviors by using the time out method or withdrawing playtime or a toy. Then teach what you do want by rewarding him well for obedience.

Punishment strains your relationship with your dog. It makes him fear you, not respect you. And he won't want to be your obedient little buddy if he fears you. Positive reinforcement, on the other hand, does motivate him to please you and makes him consider you his master. He will strive to please you if he knows that you will reward him for doing so.

The foundation of your training should be offering rewards for good behavior. When training your Aussie, use a dog training clicker, a treat, and plenty of praise; you will learn his preference early on. Teach him to associate obeying you with getting something good that he likes. Make sure the reward means a lot to him so that it has more power. For instance, if your dog loves the dog park, you can reward him for good behavior by saying, "Let's go to the dog park." He will soon learn what that means, associate the reward, and he will start jumping around for joy. Treats and rewards serve as powerful motivators. Above all, always show love to your Miniature Australian Shepherd. Praise him just for lying there or for being your friend. Dog's love hearing that they are good boys. Showing your Australian Shepherd lots of love will create and cement an amazing loving bond between you two for life.

Consistency Is the Key

The other crucial part of your Aussie training foundation is consistency. You want to always offer a consequence for each thing that your dog does. Bad behavior is never tolerated or condoned. Good behavior is always rewarded.

You need to be consistent with your commands. Pick a command and process that works well, and stick to it. Switching up commands will confuse your dog because he will not know what you want.

Finally, a consistent schedule is ideal for your dog's sense of wellbeing and calm. You will have better luck training him if you train at consistent times, as well as to feed, exercise, groom, and play at consistent times. He will get used to his schedule and will know what to expect. This helps him calm down so that he is more open to learning and being a good boy.

Secrets of Potty Training

House training should start when you immediately bring your Aussie home. Don't wait, or he will get stuck in bad habits. You can start potty training your Australian Shepherd at any age, though, of course, it is ideal to start when your dog is a puppy, and moreover at the age and times suggested herein. The minute your furry friend enters your home, he needs to understand that this is where the pack lives. Give him a tour, prevent marking whilst touring his new surroundings and home.

One problem with puppies pooping and peeing is that they must pee every hour, and pooping happens more often in puppies than adult dogs. You will get messes in the house if you don't provide your pup with adequate pee breaks. On top of that, he does not yet understand that going inside is a puppy dog no-no. Be sure to let him outside every hour and guide him to a specific place on your property to take care of his business. When he does his business outside, really praise him. Show him that peeing and pooping outside is good behavior.

Some dogs also like to go inside the house to mark their territory. This may especially be a problem with male dogs who are not neutered or who were neutered late in life. The problem can also be compounded if you have other dogs present in the house. It is all about territory for dogs; they don't see it as ruining furniture; they see it as claiming that furniture for themselves. You can use a hormone spray to keep your dogs from wanting to pee on the furniture. While scolding your dog for doing his business inside is hardly effective, you can teach him some commands like "go outside" or "no" when you spy him trying to lift his leg on your new couch. Remove him from the furniture and take him outside to his pre-designated place for relieving himself whenever you catch him trying to mark his territory indoors.

Start by determining an evacuation spot where your dog is welcome to go to the bathroom. Take him to this spot whenever you think he needs to go. Say "Potty time" to teach him that this is a command. Whenever he evacuates in his designated spot, really praise him. You can even use a clicker. Click when he goes and offer him a treat.

Take him out to his spot on a reliable schedule. For little puppies, this is forty-five minutes to an hour. For puppies four months and up, every four hours is OK. For adult dogs, you can go five hours if you must, though four hours is most recommended for your dog.

Try to teach him to tell you when he needs to go out. Not all dogs naturally whine at the door. Hang a little bell by your door and put some cheese or peanut butter on it. Every time he licks it, and it rings, take him out to his designated potty spot. This forms the association in his mind between the bell ringing and going outside. When he needs to use the potty spot, he will know to ring the bell.

Secrets to Leash Training Your Aussie

First, you want to select a good leash. Use a head leash for big powerful dogs who want to walk you. Front or head attachment leashes are also great choices. Try to select a leash with less than six feet of length. This prevents your dog from having the room to lunge out and potentially hurt himself if he sees something that he wants to chase.

Start in the backyard to get him used to be on a leash. Choose which side you want to walk him on and stay consistent with that side. Usually on your left side, but either side is fine. Both sides, even better. As he walks beside you, reward him. Feed him a treat at your thigh level and use the word "Heel" when he is approaching your side and before the treating When repeated enough times, he will learn to like staying by your thigh when you say the command word "Heel" because this is where he knows he gets his treats.

Try going at different paces. Make sure that you only reward your dog when he heels or walks right alongside you at your pace. If he lags or bounds ahead, don't reward him. If he gets distracted, say "Heel" and slap your thigh with the leash to get his attention. He will run to join you. Then reward him. Also, increase the increments of time between rewards as he learns to walk alongside you obediently.

Now you can try taking your Australian Shepherd out on the leash. Reward him when he keeps pace with you at your thigh. When he tries to pull and run ahead of you, simply turn the other way. Reward him with a click and treat when he falls into step beside you again. Also, continue to teach him to "Heel" and guide him to walk alongside you at a pace matching yours.

You are the leader, and you want to establish that. He can only go where you want to go and walk as fast as you want to walk. This makes walking your dog a fun and relaxing exercise for both of you and all you encounter on your merry way.

CHAPTER 8:

Physical and Mental Exercise

No matter your Australian Shepherd's age, bonding with him is one of the key steps in training him perfectly. As soon as you take your Aussie puppy or adult dog home, the first thing you should do is develop a loving and caring bond with him, so he can trust you, especially if he is from a shelter or rescue group.

Make sure you win his confidence and trust; do not push him too hard; keep being your loving self and let him come to you, which he will, as an Australian shepherd love to be with their owner at all times.

Give him lots of praise and treats.

When your Aussie knows that he belongs with you and your family, he will react better to the commands and training.

If you crave respect and trust from him, then it is a two-way street to make sure you trust and also respect him.

Golden Rules to Develop a Strong Bond With Your Aussie

Quality Time

To develop a stronger bond with your Australian Shepherd, make sure you spend quality time with him. Take him out with you on cycling, walks, and bike rides, and car rides.

Reward Behavior

Praising your Aussie is equally as important as giving him treats. Showing affection is healthier and effective. Kind behavior, treats, cuddles, hugs are a great way to show you love and care for him. So, make him your best buddy as he will associate you with the positive experience and be much calmer and safer with you.

Safe Environment

Create a safe and calm environment; consistency is the crucial step in your Australian shepherd life. Provide him with an environment that is safe to explore and is his haven. This is such an important step for shelter and rescue dogs as his prior life may not have been as calm and safe; when he looks at you, he should feel that your home is as safe as it can get. Provide him with fresh water and healthy food at the same time each day, develop a routine to groom him, and for other tasks. The bond between you two will be stronger than ever.

Before making your Australian Shepherd understand what you want from him, also try to understand his behavior. There are activities and sports you can play with him, which will strengthen your bond with your Aussie. Moreover, do not force him to play with you, even though he will always be ready to let him come to you.

Frisbee Activity

Australian Shepherd loves to play games; you should try playing Frisbee with him. There are many Frisbees available in the market of different vibrant colors and shapes. Some even serve as a chew toy for your Aussie. If you have a puppy, then get the chew toy one but if he is out of the chewing phase, get the classic Frisbee that can go a long way as Aussies love to run for a long time. Take him to your yard or a dog park where you are not worried about him getting too far away. No matter the weather, your Australian Shepherd will love to play with you.

Treat Finding

On those days where you do not feel like going out much, you can play hide the treats and ask your Australian Shepherd to look for them around the place or the backyard. Make sure he does not turn the place upside down. Learn to give him commands in between if he gets too excited. When he finds the treats make sure to praise him.

Movie Night

Put on an animated movie with vibrant colors and other animals. If your Aussie shows interest in the movie, enjoy with him. Give him lots of cuddles during the move time, and he will be the happiest pet, which works in your favor.

Training

Make training for you and your Australian Shepherd a fun experience. With lots of praising and treats, teach him a new trick, teach him to balance a biscuit on his nose.

Box Fun

Get a box made of cardboard that is big enough to fit your Australian Shepherd. Get yourself a clicker and some of his favorite treats.

Place the box on the floor. It will get your Australian Shepherd's attention. As soon as he comes near the box, he nudges it, gets the clicker sound on, and gives him treats. Gradually your Aussie will learn if he interacts with the box, he will get the goodies, so your Aussie will try to nudge it more; maybe he will try to sit in it. It will get him trained with the clicker, and treats will make him happy, and the curiosity will occupy his mind.

Kong Toys

You can play games with the Kong toy. It is such a versatile toy and will keep your Australian Shepherd busy. Fill the Kong with canned dog food, peanut butter, or other of his favorite food, freeze and play fetch with it.

Your Australian Shepherd will love it and keep occupied.

Hiking and Running

Hiking is a great way for your Australian Shepherd to burn energy and for you to get fit and healthy. Take him hiking and running with you; let him observe, play, and explore the surroundings as they make a fun partner for running and hiking. But, make sure your Australian Shepherd has developed into an adult. Do not take your Aussie puppies on hiking or extreme running.

Agility

As we know by now, a tired Australian shepherd is the happiest pet. So, set up agility like an obstacle in your house but, of course, keep them short due to space. Let him have at it, and do not forget to reward him throughout activities.

CHAPTER 9:

Dog Language

We all know good communication is not just about the words we use; our tone of voice, energy, and body language help to package up and deliver our meaning every day. While most people can effectively communicate their thoughts and feelings through words, we need to generally be reliant upon reading our dog's body language in order to know if they are happy, sad, nervous, or aggressive.

How happy would you be if you could not communicate with your family at home? Would you develop behavior issues over time? Of course, you would, and the same is also true for your beloved dog.

They need you to understand what they are "telling you" and how they feel in order to be a happy family member. For instance, learning to properly "read" your dog's intentions can easily prevent an unwanted encounter during a visit to the local park.

Therefore, taking the time to educate yourself about basic canine body language and paying attention to your dog's body language (including their face, posture, barking, and tail position) is an important prerequisite for raising a well-behaved content dog.

This segment will teach you exactly that—to understand the basics of what your furry friend (and those dogs around you) are trying to "tell" you and how they feel so that you can share a happy lifelong partnership together.

So, don't wait because now is a good time to start developing and honing your canine body language skills.

All the Wagging and Barking

While a well-socialized Australian Shepherd may often happily wag their tail (if they have one), it can be a mistake to automatically assume that if your dog, or someone else's dog, is wagging their tail, they are happy and friendly.

What the Wag Means

When determining a dog's true intent or demeanor, it's important to take into consideration the complete dog posture, rather than just the tail, because it's entirely possible that a dog can be wagging his or her tail just before it decides to take an aggressive lunge toward you or your dog.

More important in determining the emotional state of most dogs is the height or positioning of their tail. For instance, a tail that is held parallel to your dog's back usually suggests that they are feeling relaxed, whereas if the tail is held stiffly vertical, this usually means that they may be feeling aggressive or dominant.

Also, keep in mind that certain dog tails are carried differently for different reasons. Depending on which dog tail, you will have more or less visible cues. The opposite is also true of other dogs reading your dog's body language. For instance, a dog with a docked or tightly curled tail can sometimes send confusing messages to others.

A tail held much lower can mean that your dog is feeling stressed, afraid, submissive, or unwell, and if the tail is tucked underneath the dog's body, this is most often a sign that the dog is feeling highly stressed, nervous, fearful, or threatened by another dog, person or unfamiliar situation.

Paying attention to your dog's tail (and any dog tails around you) can help you to know when you need to step in and make some space between your dog and another, more dominant or nervous dog.

Of course, different breeds naturally carry their tails at different heights, some dogs have tightly curled tails, and some dogs (like the Aussie) may not have any visible tails. You will need to take this into consideration so that you get used to their particular body language signals.

Likewise, the speed at which the tail is moving will give you an idea of the mental state of your dog; the speed of the wag usually indicates how excited a dog may be.

For instance, a slow, slightly swinging wag can often mean that a dog is tentative about greeting another dog, and this is more of a questioning type of wag, whereas a fast-moving tail held high can mean that your dog is about to challenge or threaten another less dominant dog.

Also, a stalking stance, where a dog has raised hackles (hair along the back), lowers its head, crouches, and slowly creeps forward with an intense stare, often happens just before a serious attack. There is also a similar-looking "play" stance, and without practice, you may have difficulty identifying the difference between the two.

What the Bark Means

Of course, our dogs bark for a wide variety of reasons, and every dog is different, depending upon their natural breed tendencies and how they were raised. In the case of the Australian Shepherd, while barking may be part of their herding style, you can certainly teach them not to bark unless absolutely necessary. Here are some of the more common reasons why a dog might be barking.

Communication

Since the very first dog, they have communicated over long distances by howling to one another and when in closer proximity. They tend to bark to warn off other dogs are approaching what they consider to be their territory, or in excitement or happiness when greeting another member of the dog pack.

Now, our domesticated dogs have learned to bark for a wide variety of reasons, such as when they sense danger or are alerting us to someone approaching the home. A dog will also bark in anticipation of their favorite food when they are afraid, frustrated, bored, excited, or to let us know they want to play. Barking is an effective way to get the attention of us humans because barking is a loud and difficult noise to ignore.

Danger

Many dogs will bark to alert us to visitors or intruders, and we need to learn how to understand the difference between what our dogs perceive as dangerous and what is truly dangerous, or indeed how to teach our best friends the difference.

We want our dogs to tell us when there is real, imminent danger, and in this case, should the danger involve an unwanted intruder, we want them to bark loudly to possibly scare this threat away.

When our dogs are barking for a reason we are not yet aware of; we need to assess the situation rather than immediately becoming annoyed calmly.

We also need to remember that an Australian Shepherd's sense of smell, hearing, and sometimes eyesight is far more acute than our own, which means that we need to give them an opportunity to tell us if they just heard, saw, or sensed something that they are worried or uncertain about.

Rather than ignoring our dogs (or yelling at them) when they are attempting to "tell" us that something is bothering them, even if we ourselves understand that the noise the dog just heard is only the neighbor's kids coming home from school or postal delivery, we need to respond appropriately.

We need to calmly acknowledge our dog's concern by saying, "OK, good dog," and then ask them to come to you. This way, you have quietly and calmly let your dog know that the situation is nothing to be concerned about, and you have asked them to move away from the target they are concerned about, which places you in control, and which will usually stop the barking.

Attention

Many dogs will learn to bark to get their owner's attention, just because they are bored or want to be taken outside for an interesting walk or a trip to the local park to chase a ball.

Our canine companions are very good at manipulating us in this way, and if we fall for it, we are setting up an annoying precedent that could plague us for the remainder of our relationship.

When a dog is barking to gain its guardian's attention, for whatever reason, before we immediately capitulate, first we need to ask our dog to make eye contact with us calmly and do something we ask of them. After our dog has performed a calm and quiet task for us, such as sit or lie down, then we can decide to give our dog our undivided attention on our terms.

Often you will see a dog and its guardian at the local dog park playing fetch, and when the human is not throwing that ball quickly enough to satisfy the dog's desire to run and fetch, the dog will be madly barking at the guardian. This is the equivalent of being sworn at in doggy language.

Don't make the mistake of allowing your puppy or dog to manipulate you in this situation because if you do, you will soon create a bad habit that will very quickly become not just annoying to you but also annoying to everyone else at the park.

Before throwing a ball or Frisbee for a dog that loves to retrieve, it's important always to ask the dog to sit and make eye contact with you.

Often the types of canines that are overly exuberant with chasing a ball or Frisbee (such as the Australian Shepherd) have learned this barking behavior from their humans, who allowed themselves to be literally at the beck and call of their dog and created this irritating habit by throwing the ball every time the dog barked.

In this situation, if you allow your dog to dictate to you when you will throw the ball, they will quickly learn that barking gets them their desired result, and you have just created an annoying, rude dog who is yelling at you in doggy language to do their bidding.

In this type of ball-retrieving scenario, the dog has become ball "obsessed" and is no longer really paying attention to the guardian's commands, as they are solely focusing on where the ball is.

While there are many situations in which your dog may bark to convey that they've heard a noise, in all other situations where the barking is done to demand attention, a toy, another object, or food, this is when you need to ask them to do something for you, and then only if you want to give them what they are asking for, do you follow through.

Bottom line, remember to stay calm when your cute puppy is demanding attention because even negative attention can be rewarding for your dog and can lead down a future, unwanted path where he or she will learn further habits that will not be particularly endearing for the human side of the relationship when the cute puppy has become an adult.

Boredom or Separation Anxiety

Many dogs, especially those who have not been properly trained, are treated like children, are under-exercised, or have not been allowed to understand that they have rules and boundaries, will sharply bark when left at home, and are bored, or are feeling the anxiety of being alone.

Many times, we humans believe that our dog is barking when being left alone because he or she is experiencing "separation anxiety," when in fact, what the dog is really experiencing is the frustration of observing a member of the pack which they believe to be their follower (i.e., You) leaving them.

This can happen when you are not a strong enough leader for your very smart Australian Shepherd, and he or she has taken over. They may then loudly verbalize their frustration and displeasure because, in the dog world, the pack follower (which you have allowed yourself to be) does NOT leave the pack leader (them). I've seen this type of situation many times over, and once the human side of the relationship steps up and takes control, it quickly reverses.

Breaking your dog of the habit of loud barking when they are left alone can be solved in different ways, with the most obvious being that you simply take your dog with you wherever you go, because after all, they are pack animals, and in order for them to be really happy and well balanced, they need the constant direction of their leader (which is supposed to be you).

Another much lengthier and time-consuming way to solve a barking problem could involve hiring a professional to help assess why the problem has occurred in the first place and then devise an effective plan to reverse the problem that will work for each unique situation.

Fear or Pain

Another reason your dog may bark is when they are very frightened or in pain, and this is usually a type of bark that sounds quite different from all the others, often being a combination of a bark and a whine or a yelping type of noise.

This is a bark that you will want to pay close attention to so that you can quickly respond and offer the assistance that your puppy or dog may need.

Whatever reason your dog may be barking for, always remember that this is how they communicate and "tell" us that they want something or are concerned, afraid, nervous or unhappy about something, and as their guardians, we humans need to pay attention.

Raised Hackles

When your dog approaches with raised hackles (the hair along the dog's back), while this can be an indication that the dog may be approaching with dominant or aggressive tendencies, it also may be an indication that he or she is excited, fearful, startled, anxious or lacks confidence.

In any of these circumstances (whether it's your dog or someone else's), it's a good idea to be respectful and keep your distance until you can assess what's really going on because even a reactive, fearful dog can quickly turn into a biting dog, and I can tell you from personal experience that being bitten by any dog really hurts.

Learning your Australian Shepherd's particular body language can take some time, and we will help you get started. The more you are out and about with your dog, visiting and socializing in local parks and going on walks where you will find other dogs, animals, and people to observe, the more opportunity you will have to become skilled at recognizing the many subtleties of dog body language. Paying attention to your Aussie's verbal and body-language signals, as explained above, will help you figure out what message they are trying to get across to you, and this can make all the difference in preventing frustration for you both while raising a happy and well-behaved dog.

One last thought about body language and energy—check-in with yourself before you walk out the door with your dog, because if you're not in the moment and have your mind on something that has nothing to do with having a successful and pleasant walk with your dog, you may be setting yourself up for trouble.

For example, if you go out the door with your dog while displaying sad, weak, fearful, or confusing energy, your dog will pick up on this and become nervous or confused because your energy is no longer conveying to your dog that you are their leader. This means that your energy can literally be the cause of, for instance, an uncomfortable encounter with another person walking their dog.

It's very important to keep in mind that when walking with a dog, the moment they sense that you are not completely in control, they will take this unspoken "cue" from you that being in charge has now defaulted to him or her.

You must never allow any dog to feel they must protect you from the postman, neighbor's cat, or that taunting little terrier walking across the street, because if they do, you're literally out walking with a highly unpredictable, live "weapon" that could decide to go off at any moment.

Most Australian Shepherds can be trained to accept other dogs, animals, and unknown people, if you have put in the time and properly socialized and trained them.

However, should you let your dog get seriously out of control, you could end up with a lawsuit on your hands and/or sky-high veterinary bills if this companion is forced into being confrontational with another dog, and that's if you're lucky.

It's always a good idea to keep in mind that if your dog harms another dog, animal, or person, the consequences could be far worse than a high vet bill. For instance, any dog that bites could face a death sentence or a ruling that they can never be seen in public unless they're wearing a muzzle.

CHAPTER 10:

Hand Cues

Learn special hand cues to use with or without your verbal commands

The Usefulness of Hand Cues

Here's why. You can use hand cues in addition to your verbal commands or separately. The handy part; say you're on your phone working from home while in an important conversation. You wouldn't want to say, "Hold on, I need my dog to sit." Instead, you could give the "Sit" hand cue without verbalizing the command while continuing your discussion. Pretty handy, huh?

"Sit" Hand Cue

To get your dog to sit on his hairy fanny, you want to hold up your hand with your palm facing toward your dog. Similar to making the Stop sign.

Start training by having your dog sit down. Reward him with a click and a small treat. Now try this again and tell him to "sit" while using the hand cue and click and treat. Practice this at least fifteen times. At this point, you are ready to try using the hand cue without a verbal command. Hold your hand up until he sits and then click and reward. You may have to make him sit with your hands to reaffirm the notion of what you are doing. Practice this at least fifteen times. Now change the context up a bit and begin practicing this in different locations, like the yard and out in public.

"Stay" Hand Cue

Holding your fist up may indicate power to we humans, but to your dog, this will mean "Stay." He should stop moving as soon as he sees this gesture and stay exactly where it is. Curl your fingers into a fist and hold it up with your palm toward your dog. Start training by giving your dog his "Stay" verbal command. Reward him with a click and a small treat. Now try this again and tell him to "Stay" while using the hand cue and click and treat only when he stays in place. Practice this combination fifteen times. Each time a few seconds more in length. At this point, you are ready to try using the hand cue without a verbal command. Hold your fist up until he sits and stays, and then hold it for a few seconds and click and reward. Then practice this hand cue fifteen times and start to increase the Stay-time by small increments until he is able to stay in place for a full minute. Reward him when he does this without any verbal command. Now change the context up a bit and begin practicing this in different locations, like the yard and out in public.

"Down" Hand Cue

The down hand cue is self-explanatory because, basically, you are making a down motion from an outward flat position. Hold your hand in an outward position, with your natural bend, while your palm is facing the floor, and make a lowering motion with your fingers and arm to a half-closed position. When successful, your dog will immediately lie down when seeing this. Start training by having your dog lay down with a verbal command. Reward him with a click and a small treat. Now try this again and tell him "Down" while using the hand cue and click and treat. Practice this at least fifteen times. At this point, you are ready to try using the hand cue without a verbal command. Hold your hand in this downward motion until he sits, then click and reward. You may have to make him lie down with your hands to reaffirm the notion of what you are doing. Practice fifteen times. Begin practicing this in different locations, like the yard and out in public. Reward when he follows the hand cue without needing a verbal command.

"Leave it" Hand Cue

A semi toward and downward point with your index finger is how you command your dog to leave something alone or mind his own business. If he is starting to mess with food, an animal, a hole he likes to dig, your shoes, etc., you will use this point to let him know to leave well enough alone. Train "Leave it" first with a verbal command when he messes with something he shouldn't. When he drops it, reward him with a click and a small treat. Next, give him a toy or bone he enjoys messing with, tell him "Leave it" while using the hand cue, click, treat when he obeys. Practice this command fifteen times. At this point, you are ready to try using the hand cue without a verbal command. Point until he leaves it, click and treat. You may have to make him leave it with your hands to reaffirm the action. Keep practicing this at least fifteen times. Change the places up and begin practicing this in different public locations. Reward when he follows the hand cue without needing a verbal command.

"Quiet" Hand Cue

Making the OK hand cue is a good way to tell your dog to hush when he is barking or braying. When he sees this signal, he will know to fall quiet.

Start training by having your dog quiet down with a verbal command. Reward him with a click and a small treat. Now try this again and tell him "Quiet" while using the hand cue, click and treat. Practice this command fifteen times.

Now you are ready to try using the hand cue without a verbal command. Hold the "OK" signal until he stops barking and then click and treat. Practice this at least fifteen times.

Change the context up a bit and begin practicing this in different locations, like the yard and out in public. Always reward when he does what you want and responds to the hand cue without needing a verbal command.

"Come" Hand Cue

"Come" is formed by holding your hand palm up, with your fingers bent. Then wiggle your aligned fingers in a back-and-forth motion to let your dog know to approach you.

Start training by having your dog "Come" with a verbal command. Reward him with a click and a small treat. Now try this again and tell him "Come" while using the hand cue and click and treat.

Practice this at least fifteen times. At this point, you are ready to try using the hand cue without a verbal command. Beckon to him with this hand signal until he comes and then click and reward. Keep practicing this at least fifteen times. Finally, change the context up a bit and begin practicing this in different locations, like the yard and out in public. Always reward when he does what you want and responds to the hand cue without needing a verbal command.

"Good Boy" Hand Cue

"Good boy" is simply a thumb's up to show your dog that he is doing what you want. Rewarding him with this hand cue can be important to encourage him to continue the desired behavior. Start training by always giving this hand signal to your dog when he obeys or behaves well, but follow up with verbal praise. Then move on to using it without verbal praise after a few times and give him a click and a treat whenever he obeys you. He will quickly learn to associate the thumbs up with being a good boy and getting a treat.

CHAPTER 11:

The Basic Commands

There are many basic commands that you will want to teach your dog. Choose a quiet place to work with your dog for no longer than twenty minutes each time you train a command. Start training early. You can train on a leash at first for greater control, then move on to training without a leash once he starts to follow basic commands with little hesitation.

Sit

Sit is one of the first commands you should teach your Aussie. When he sits on his own, tell him "Good sit" and click and treat. Then start to work with him by having him sit for you. The minute his hairy fanny touches the floor, click and treat. You may have to show him the movement by pushing his rump to the floor, but always click and treat the minute he sits down.

Come

A good dog comes when called. Start by telling your Australian Shepherd to come while bribing him with a treat. He only gets the treat when he comes all the way to you. Now start to say "Come" in a variety of settings, particularly in situations where he is busy playing or is occupied with a toy. Only reward him when he comes to you. If he ignores you, repeat the command until he does. Eventually, phase out treats and expect him to come to you when called, no matter what.

Down

Wait till your puppy Aussie dog is lying down naturally and click and treat him while telling him, "Good, lie down." Whenever you see your dog lying down, say "Down." Teach him what the command means before you use it in training. Once you are sure that he knows what "Down" means, you can start to use this command and tell him to lie down. Click and treat whenever he lies down at your command.

Start taking him outside and practice this in a variety of different areas. Teach him that no matter where you tell him to lie down, he only gets a click and a treat if he complies. Gradually phase out treats and clicks over time as he gets comfortable lying down when you say so.

Stay

Teach "stay" by having your best friend sit. When he is sitting, wait a few seconds before you click and treat. Do this many times, extending the amount of time that your dog must sit there waiting. Then start by saying "Stay" and hold a flat palm to his face when he sits. Wait a few seconds, and then click and treat if he stays still. If he comes toward you, start over again without reward. He must stay sitting still to get his treat. When your pup gets better at staying for up to a minute at a time, you can take it to the next level. Walk a few steps backward while telling him to "Stay." He will naturally want to get up and come to you. Direct him back to his spot and repeat the "Stay" command with your hand signal. Keep walking away. Only treat your Aussie when he sits still as long as you desire. Work your way up to two-minute increments of time between sitting and treating. Also, start to practice things like telling him to stay and then leaving his line of sight or even leaving the room. Reward him richly with praise and a treat when he stays. Or repeat when your Australian Shepherd does not comply.

Fetch

Start by playing with a toy that your dog loves. When you throw it, tell him, "Fetch!" Click and reward only when he gets the item and brings it back to you. Soon, he will learn to do this for any item whenever you say "Fetch" because he expects a reward. Point at something and say "Fetch" to teach him to use this command in any situation. Always click and reward. Phase that out as your Aussie becomes more proficient at fetching.

Drop It

When your puppy has something undesirable in his mouth, you can teach him to drop it the minute you tell him to do so. First, give him a toy that he likes. As he plays with it, hold a treat to his nose and say, "Drop it." He will drop the toy to get the treat. That's when you click and reward him.

Now start to conceal the treats. Practice this command ten times a day until he is willing to drop something for a treat that he cannot see. Eventually, you can phase out treats, and he will drop something the minute you tell him to.

Leave It

The idea behind this command is that your dog will not eat or touch things that you don't want him to. For instance, you can get him to leave roadkill alone while on walks or stop focusing on that dead-eyed rabbit staring right at him like dinner is served, or to stop chewing on something you don't want him to destroy.

First, have two treats in both hands. Let him sniff one of your hands. Next, he starts to lose interest because it's apparent he won't get the treat. Click and treat him using the other hand.

Open your hand and show him the treat. Close your hand when he tries to get it. Repeat until he ignores this hand, knowing he won't get the treat. When he finally ignores it, it's time to click and treat with the other hand. You can also say "Leave it" when he pays attention to this hand to condition him to learn the command.

Take it to the next level by placing the treat in your open hand on the floor. He will run for it. Cover it with your hand and say, "Leave it." When he starts to ignore that hand covering the treat, click and reward him. Now uncover the treat and stand up. Tell him "Leave it" and reward him with a treat from the other hand if he does.

Start to practice this in a variety of settings. Do it while walking him or while playing in the yard or neighborhood park. Tell him to leave toys he is playing with or treats that you drop on the floor.

CHAPTER 12:

Positive Reinforcement

It is always better to reward your Aussie instead of punishing him or her. Here are a few reasons why:

- If you punish your dog, it can make him distrust or cause fear, aggression, and avoidance of you. If you rub your dog's nose his doodie or pee, he may avoid going to the bathroom in front of you. This is going to make his public life difficult.
- Physical punishment has the tendency to escalate in severity. If you get your dog's attention by a light tap on the nose, he will soon get used to that and ignore it. Shortly the contact will become more and more violent. As we know, violence is not the answer.
- Punishing your dog may have some bad side effects. For example, if you are using a pinch collar, it may tighten when he encounters other dogs. Dogs are very smart, but they are not always logical. When your dog encounters another dog, the pinching of the collar may lead him to think that the other dog is the reason for

the pinch. Pinch collars have been linked to the reinforcement of aggressive behaviors between dogs.
- Electric fences will make him avoid the yard.
- Choke collars can cause injuries to a dog's throat as well as cause back and neck misalignment.
- You may inadvertently develop an adversarial relationship with your dog if you punish your dog instead of working through a reward system and correctly leading. If you only look for the mistakes within your dog, this is all you will begin to see. In your mind, you will see a problem dog. In your dog's mind, he will see anger and distrust.
- You ultimately want to shape your dog's incorrect actions into acceptable actions. By punishing your dog, he will learn only to avoid punishment. He is not learning to change the behavior you want to be changed; instead, he learns to be sneaky or to do the very minimum to avoid being punished. Your dog can become withdrawn and seemingly inactive. Permanent psychological damage can be done if a dog lives in fear of punishment.
- If you punish rather than reward, neither you nor your dog will be having a very good time. It will be a constant, sometimes painful struggle. If you have children, they will not be able to participate in a

punishment-based training process because it is too difficult and truly not fun.

- Simply put, if you train your dog using rewards, you and your dog will have a much better time and relationship. Rely on rewards to change his behavior by using treats, toys, playing, petting, affection, or anything else you know your dog likes. If your dog is doing something that you do not like, replace the habit with another by teaching your dog to do something different, and then reward him or her for doing the replacement action, and then you can all enjoy the outcome.

Treats

You are training your puppy, and it is going well because your pup is the best dog in the world. Oh yes, he is; everyone knows this to be true. Because of this fact, you want to make sure that you are giving your dog the right type of treats.

Treats are easy, as long as you stay away from the things that aren't good for dogs, such as; avocados, onions, garlic, coffee, tea, caffeinated drinks, grapes, raisins, macadamia nuts, peaches, plums, pits, seeds, persimmons, and chocolates.

Dog owners can make treats from many different foods. Treats should always be sized about the dimension of a kernel of corn. This makes them easy to grab from treat pouches and still flavorful enough for your hound to desire them.

All a dog needs are a little taste to keep them interested. The kernel size is something that is swiftly eaten and swallowed, thus not distracting from the training session. A treat is only to provide a quick taste, used for enticement and reinforcement, not as a snack or meal.

When you are outdoors, and there are many distractions, treats should be of a higher quality that is coveted by your pooch. Trainers call it a higher value treat because it is worthy of your dog breaking away from the activity they are engaged in. Perhaps cubes of cheese, dried, or cooked meats will qualify as your dog's high-value treat.

Make sure you mix up the types of treats by keeping a variety of them available. Nothing is worse during training than when your puppy turns his nose up at a treat because he has grown bored of it or it happens to be of lesser value than his interests hold.

Types of Treats

Human foods that are safe for dogs include most fruits and veggies, cut-up meats that are raw or cooked, yogurt, peanut butter, kibble, and whatever else you discover that your dogs like, but be sure that it is good for them, in particular their digestive system. Be advised that not all human foods are good for dogs. Please read about human foods that are acceptable for dogs and observe your dog's stools when introducing new ideas for treats.

How many times have you heard a friend or family member tell you about some crazy food that their dog loves? Dogs do love a massive variety of foods; unfortunately, not all of the foods that they think they want to eat are good for them. Dog treating is not rocket science, but it does take a little research, common sense, and paying attention to how your dog reacts after wolfing down a treat.

Many people like to make homemade treats, and that is okay. Just keep to the rules we just mentioned and watch what you are adding while having fun in the kitchen. Remember to research and read the list of vegetables that dogs can and cannot eat, and understand that pits and seeds can cause choking and intestinal issues, such as dreaded doggy flatulence. When preparing, first remove any seeds and pits, and clean all fruits and veggies before slicing them into doggie size treats.

Before purchasing treats, look at the ingredients on the treat packaging, and be sure there are no chemicals, fillers, additives, colors, and things that are unhealthy. Some human foods that are tasty to us might not be so tasty to your dog, and he will let you know. Almost all dogs love some type of raw or cooked meat. In tiny nibble sizes, these treats work great at directing their attention where you want it focused. Here are some treat ideas:

- Whole grain cereals, such as cheerios without sugar added are a good choice.
- Kibble (dry foods). Put some in a paper bag and boost the aroma factor by tossing in some bacon or another meat product. Dogs are all about those yummy smell sensations.
- Beef jerky that has no pepper or heavy seasoning added.
- Carrots, apple pieces, and some dogs even enjoy melons.
- Meats that have been cubed and are not highly processed or salted are easy to make at home as well. You can use cooked left-over foods.

- Shredded cheese, string cheese, or cubed cheese; dogs love cheese!
- Cream cheese, peanut butter, or spray cheese, give your dog a small dollop to lick for every proper behavior. These work well when training puppies to ring a bell to go outside for evacuation.
- Baby food meat products certainly don't look yummy to us, but dogs adore them.
- Ice cubes, but if your dog has dental problems, proceed cautiously.
- Commercial dog treats, but use caution; there are loads of them on the market. Look for those that do not have preservatives, by-products, or artificial colors. Additionally, take into consideration the country of origin.

Never feed or treat your four-legged friend from the dining table because you do not want to teach that begging actions are acceptable. When treating, give treats far from the dinner table or from areas that people normally gather to eat, such as by the BBQ.

How and When to Treat

The best time to issue dog treats is between meals. Treating close to mealtimes makes all treats less effective, so remember this when planning your training sessions. If during training you need to refocus your dog back into the training session, keep a high-value treat in reserve.

Obviously, if your dog is full from mealtime, he will be less likely to want a treat reward than if a bit hungry. If your dog is not hungry, your training sessions will likely be more difficult and far less effective. This is why it is a good idea to reward correct actions with praise, play, or toys and not to rely exclusively on treats.

- Love and attention are considered rewards and are certainly positive reinforcement that can be just as effective as an edible treat. Dog treating is comprised of edibles, praise, and attention. Engaging in play or allowing some quality time with their favorite rope toy is also effective. At times, these treats are crucial to dog training.
- Do not give your dog a treat without asking for action first. Say, "sit," and after your dog complies, deliver the treat. This reinforces your training and their obedience.
- Avoid treating your dog when he is overstimulated and running amuck in an unfocused state of mind. This can be counterproductive and might reinforce a negative behavior resulting in the inability to get your dog's attention.

- Due to their keen sense of smell, they will know long before you could ever know that there is a tasty snack nearby, but keep it out of sight. Issue your command and wait for your dog to obey before presenting the reward. Remember, when dog treating, it is important to be patient and loving, but it is equally important not to give the treat until your dog obeys.

- Some dogs have a natural gentleness and always take from your hand gently, while other dogs need some guidance to achieve this. If your dog is a bit rough during treat grabbing, go ahead and train the command "gentle!" when giving treats. Be firm from this point forward. Give no treats unless they are gently taken from your hand. Remain steadfast with your decision to implement this, and soon your pup will comply if he wants the tasty treat.

Bribery vs. Reward Dog Treating

The other day a friend of mine mentioned bribing for an action that he had commanded. I thought about it later and thought I would clarify for my readers. Bribery is the act of offering the food visually in advance so that the dog will act out a command or alter behavior. The reward is giving your dog his favorite toy, treat, love, or affection after he has performed the commanded action.

An example of bribery would happen when you want your dog to come, and before you call your dog, you hold a cube of steak for them to see. The reward would be giving your dog the steak after they have obeyed the come command. Never show the treats before issuing commands.

Bribed dogs learn to comply with your wishes only when they see food. The rewarded dog realizes that they only receive treats after performing the desired actions. This also assists by introducing non-food items as prizes when training and treating.

CHAPTER 13:

Negative Reinforcement

In training your Australian Shepherd, negative reinforcement is a tool, just like reward and positive reinforcement. Let's take an in-depth look at how negative reinforcement works.

In order to understand this concept, you first need to understand what it means for something to be aversive or punishing. Something aversive is anything that the canine finds unpleasant or painful—these events are typically called "punishments." Some examples of punishments are being yelled at, spanked, hit with a rolled-up newspaper, being left outside, and not getting fed for many hours. Punishments can also be things that the pup has found unpleasant in the past (e.g., thunderstorms). When we use negative reinforcement, then we are trying to create a situation that the dog finds unpleasant.

Here's an example of how negative reinforcement works. Let's say that your Australian Shepherd is playing frisbee with her friend—that's fun! But then she decides to run off to chase a cat. You tell her "no" and give her a sharp swat on the butt. That hurts—she didn't like that, and it made her stop chasing the cat. So, she figures out that if she wants to stop being hurt by you, she needs to stop chasing the cat. This process is negative reinforcement. You hurt her (the punishment) when she's doing something wrong (in this case, chasing the cat), so she figures out that if she doesn't want to be hurt, she should stop doing the wrong thing.

Positive reinforcement works in a more straightforward way. Let's say that you're outside in the yard, and your Aussie starts barking at a neighboring dog. You tell your dog "quiet," then give her lots of praise and petting when she stops barking. She wants to keep getting all of that attention, so it makes sense for her to figure out how to get it by not barking at other dogs. This is positive reinforcement; she does the right thing (in this case, not barking at the other dogs) in order to get more good stuff (praise and petting).

So far, we've only talked about how punishments and rewards work when used to train behavior. But what about with a puppy? Is it ever okay to use punishment on a young dog? You bet! Punishments are an invaluable tool for puppies as well as older dogs. A puppy Aussie will never be a pleasure to walk on a leash until he's had some experience with leash corrections—a punishment for pulling ahead on the leash.

If you are going to use punishment with a puppy, it must be done properly. There are some situations where punishments might be appropriate for a puppy but not an adult Aussie (e.g., hitting your puppy). It can also sometimes be easier to use punishments when raising a puppy because he won't yet have learned how to manipulate you effectively for treats or other rewards. When using punishment, timing is crucial, and it's important that the punishment starts very soon after the wrong action occurs.

For example, let's say that you're in the backyard with your Aussie puppy, and she starts to chase the neighbor's cat. You tell her "no," turn her around, and walk away from the cat. She runs toward the cat again—you repeat your no command and walk in a different direction than the cat. She tries it a third time, but you put her in her crate without petting or saying anything to her when she realized that she wasn't getting anything for continuing to chase cats. In this case, you're punishing your puppy for continuing to chase the cat by putting her in a time-out—a punishment—when she continues to do so after giving her two chances to stop on her own.

Here's another example: you're playing with your puppy in the yard, and she starts to chase some neighborhood kids. You tell her "no"—she ignores you and runs after the kids. You grab her collar, say "no" again, and bring her back into the yard. This time, you walk over to the fence and watch her for a few minutes before letting her out of your sight again. She starts to run toward the kids again—you give a quick correction on the leash (e.g., by jerking it) so that she now knows that running toward the kids results in something unpleasant (e.g., being jerked). This time, she doesn't chase the kids. In this case, you're punishing your puppy by giving her a leash correction—a punishment, like a seat on the butt—when she continues to do something wrong after you've already told her "no."

Again, it's important to note that timing is crucial when using punishments. If you give a puppy a leash correction for jumping on the kids when she's not even in the process of lunging toward them yet, then you're just being mean. It's important that the punishment occurs very soon after the action you don't want occurs—the goal is to make sure your dog understands that if he does X, Y will happen.

Okay, so how do you actually give punishment to a puppy? The first step is to decide what kind of punishment you're going to use. There are two main types of punishments, leash corrections and time-outs. Leash corrections can be anything from a quick jerk on the leash when your puppy is misbehaving to picking her up and putting her in her crate when she isn't listening. When giving your puppy a time-out, make sure she doesn't associate it with something she already does, like eating or playing with anything.

Once you've decided what type of punishment to use, the next step is to figure out how it's going to work. Basically, if you're punishing your puppy for something she did in the past, then she needs to know that the punishment is unrelated to whatever you're trying to teach her in the future. For example, if I'm teaching my dog not to pull at leash by using a leash correction when she pulls ahead of me, and it seems like she's getting confused about what's happening—in other words, if I think she's starting to think "oh no! Here comes a jerk on the leash. Now I know to keep walking alongside my person!"—then I need to make sure that the next time she pulls, she doesn't think that the jerk on the leash is because of what she's doing, but rather because of something completely unrelated to walking such as chasing after squirrels.

The same rule applies whether you're using a time-out or a leash correction—you want to make sure your puppy doesn't get confused about why it's happening and starts to associate it with something she's already doing. To do this, you can pair your punishment with something else when you're not punishing your puppy. For example, if you're going to use a leash correction when your puppy is jumping on people, make sure that you're giving her a ton of praise and treats every time she's not jumping.

What about scolding? If you've already used a leash correction or placed your puppy in time-out for something she did wrong, and you think she's getting confused about why it happened, then sometimes it can help to give her a brief verbal punishment such as "no" right after the leash correction or when she gets out of time-out. The goal is to make sure that your puppy understands what she's done wrong.

When you're scolding your puppy after a correction/time-out, the goal is to make sure that she doesn't think that you're just scolding her because you're upset. To do this, I like to use what I call "the secret squirrel!" Right before I sold my dogs for something they did wrong; I quietly say, "I'm not mad at you. I don't need to be mad at you. You've done nothing wrong!" and then give them a treat (since they can't understand what I'm actually saying). This way, your puppy understands that you're not mad at her.

Get through the first couple of weeks at home. Your puppy now has a pretty good idea of what the rules are and what's expected of her. At this point, it's time to start asking for one thing (evacuation) and rewarding her for doing something else instead (taking her to the potty spot). In other words, you're going to ask her to do something (potty) before you reward her for doing something else (evacuation).

Asking for the behavior you want while rewarding a different behavior will make your puppy think about what she's doing and why. The very quickest way to teach your puppy is to stop rewarding behaviors that are undesirable and replace them with other desirable behaviors. It sounds like a small part of the process, but it can really make a big difference in your progress.

CHAPTER 14:

Taking Care of Your Puppy

When purchasing a dog, both first-time owners and veteran owners normally opt for buying a puppy. Purchasing a puppy will allow you to establish a good and healthy relationship with your dog and will set the foundation for a long, happy friendship. Another reason that makes a puppy so popular is the fact that they are among some of the most adorable creatures on the planet! However, caring for a new puppy is not the easiest thing. You will have to be prepared to make some huge lifestyle changes to accommodate your new puppy. The following unit is a simple and concise guide to help you care for the new canine addition to your family.

Find a Good Vet

Before purchasing your puppy, it is a good idea to research the vets in your local area. It is very important to find a highly qualified vet. The best way to find a good vet is by asking your friends, local dog walkers, local dog groomers, the breeder, and researching online. Once you purchase your new puppy, you should take it straight to your vet for a checkup. The checkup visit will make sure that your puppy is in good health and free from any serious birth defects or genetic health issues. Introducing your vet to your new dog while it is young also allows for your puppy to become familiar with the vet—this can help avoid stress during later visits. Taking your puppy to the vet straight away allows you to start a health care routine with your pet. It is important to arrange a vaccination design vet and also to discuss the best methods for control parasites (both internal and external).

Food

It is important to purchase food that is formulated specifically for puppies. A decent brand will have a statement from the Association of American Feed Control Officials (AAFCO), or your countries equivalent, on the packaging to ensure the food can fulfill your puppy's nutritional requirements. Small and medium-sized breeds can start eating adult dog food when they are between 9 and 12 months of age. Larger breeds of dogs should be fed on puppy kibbles while waiting for them to reach 2 years of age. It is important to make sure that your puppy has cool, fresh, and clean water available to them constantly.

Feeding Schedule

Puppies have a different feeding schedule to adult dogs. Their feeding schedule changes as they get older. I recommend feeding your puppy on the following schedule:

- 6 – 12 weeks old: 4 meals per day
- 3 – 6 months old: 3 meals per day
- 6 – 12 months old: 2 meals per day

Obedience Training

It is important to train your new puppy to be obedient. Obedience will allow your puppy to have a life full of positive interactions as well as forging a stronger bond between you and your pet. It is important to teach your puppy simple commands such as sit, stay, down and come. These commands will help to keep your dog safe and under control in any potentially dangerous situations. I recommend attending a local obedience training class. Obedience classes allow for you and your dog to learn the best methods for each process and command. Obedience classes also allow you, and your puppy, to interact with other people and dogs of all ages and from all backgrounds. It is important to remember that positive reinforcement has been proven to be a dramatically more effective process than punishment.

Bathroom Training

Housetraining is a priority if you want to keep your house clean! Before you start your housetraining, it is important to locate a suitable location for your puppy to go to the bathroom. If your puppy has not had all of its vaccinations it is important to find a bathroom that is inaccessible to other animals. This will help to avoid your puppy getting any unnecessary viruses or diseases.

There are three keys tricks to keep in mind when you are attempting to housetrain your puppy: positive reinforcement, planning and patience. It is important positively praise your puppy when they go to the bathroom outside and not to punish them when inevitable accidents will happen. I recommend the following times to try and introduce your puppy to a bathroom routine:

- When you first wake up.
- When your puppy wakes up from any naps it might have.
- During and after physical exercise.
- After your puppy eats or drinks a lot of water.
- Immediately before bedtime.

Be Social

The main way to avoid your puppy developing behavioral problems is to be social with it. At around 2 to 4 months old, most puppies will begin to take other animals, places, people, and involvements. It is important to start socializing your puppy with as many people and animals as possible. I recommend bringing your puppy to a dog park, to your friends or relatives houses, to dog friendly restaurants and to have other people accompany you while you walk your pet. By interacting with multiple different types of people and animals, your puppy will learn to be more social and accepting.

Signs of Illness

It is important to watch your puppy closely to make sure that it is not exhibiting any signs of illness. Your puppy is at its most vulnerable stage of its development. If you notice any of the following signs you should take your puppy to the vet immediately: lack of appetite, vomiting, lack of weight gain, lack of growth, diarrhea, pale gums, nasal discharge, inability to pass urine and stool, lethargy, swelling and difficulty breathing.

Spaying and Neutering

There are a lot of factors to considered when deciding if you should spay or neuter your puppy. Many owners refuse to spay or neuter their puppy due to the fact that they find it morally wrong and unnatural. However, most owners do decide to have their pet neutered. Shelter euthanasia is the number one killer of dogs and companion animals throughout America. In Atlanta alone over 15 million dollars is spent annually on euthanizing unwanted dogs! The only way to avoid this is to have your pet spayed or neutered. Dogs face some discomfort if they are in heat or are unable to mate. Spaying and neutering creates no long-term health problems for your pet. At the end of the day, it is an important decision for you and your family to make. I advise talking it over with your vet and family/friends who have already been through the process.

CHAPTER 15:

Socializing With People and Animals

People enjoy the taming of puppies. It can be assumed, as far as the Australian Shepherds are concerned, that this is a kind of American race used in cattle ranches. They are between 18 and 23 inches in height, and their weight is between 35 and 70 pounds. They are designed with a medium-length double coat. This coat can be straight or marcel. However, this breed can be multi-colored such as a perfect combination of red, blue merle, jet black, or red merle. Their coats are built with markings as well. As far as treatment is concerned, due care and consideration should be taken to protect them from such disorders as hip dysplasia, poor vision, deafness or blindness, etc. They should be vaccinated to shore up the strength of resistance in the body.

Before buying the Australian Shepherds, the focus should be on whether he would keep dogs at home for house security or press the dog into livestock management and animal herding. For domestic purposes, one can purchase nonchalant and polite Australian Shepherds, but dogs can be competitive and dynamic for herding livestock. There are some doubts and misunderstandings about their originality regarding the origins of the Australian Shepherds' originality. While they are considered Australian shepherds, they are probably part of the breeding line traditionally used by southern Spain's Basque shepherds. Basque shepherds had to venture to America's coasts in 1875. They were bringing these animals with them at the time. These dogs were later spread worldwide in this manner, and later they were known as Australian Shepherds by the American Kennel Club. It looks very bold and resolute. It is double coated with the round feet and straight limbs.

These puppies are very obedient to their owners. With perfection, they will track the home. This dog is very successful and professional in monitoring the property and adjacent house at night under the penetrated darkness's coverage. Therefore, nocturnal watchdogs are very successful and professional. They will also make the house owners aware of the inevitable danger. This dog has a very powerful potential for chasing. Therefore, they may be trained and pressed into action to have authority over herding livestock in the cattle ranches.

One of the most significant aspects of teaching is dog socialization. Any owner needs a well-behaved, calm, and even-tempered puppy, and with proper socialization, the road to that state begins. Exposing your dog around other persons and other pets are crucial to ensuring that he performs correctly and will help both him and you relieve tension.

The mechanism should preferably begin as early as possible for it to take root better. It is better to socialize a puppy between three and twelve weeks of age, when pups are more receptive and alert. They should get used to new circumstances at this stage in their growth and understand how they should and should not act, which are the keys to a dog's socialization.

Of course, whether you adopt an elderly dog, or your puppy had to be isolated for whatever reason when he was young, it is not always possible to initiate dog socialization that early in life. But that doesn't mean that an elderly dog can't socialize. It is always possible to socialize properly, no matter what age, provided you do it the correct way. A perfect way to start is with a morning stroll, where you can meet individuals and dogs instinctively and be able to monitor the reaction of your dog to them.

Conclusion

Congratulations! You've made it through this book, and hopefully, you're feeling like a bit of an Aussie expert by now. I hope you've enjoyed reading it and that you feel confident in selecting and raising your furry bundle of joy.

If you prefer a dog that is robust and medium-sized, possesses an adorable coat that comes in brilliant colors, is extraordinarily versatile once it is well-trained, a dog that develops through intense exercise and various athletic activities, can learn quickly and execute almost anything, a dog which is exceptionally witty; then, the perfect pick is the Australian Shepherd.

Believe me; this is not everything that there is to know about dogs. Training your Australian Shepherd is a lifelong endeavor. There are myriad other methods, tricks, tools, and things to teach and learn with your dog. You are never finished, but this is half of the fun of having a dog, as he or she is a constant work in progress. Your dog is living art.

If your training experience is anything similar to mine, there will be days and times when you think your dog will never catch on or be interested in participating and learning. I hope that you can work through the difficult times, and the result will be that you and your dog understand one another at a high level, resulting in you having command of your dog.

Owning and befriending our dogs is a lifetime adventurous commitment that is worthwhile and rewarding on every level.

Remember, it is important to learn to think like your dog. Having patience with your dog, as well as with yourself, is vital. If you do this right, you will have a relationship and a bond that will last for years. The companionship of a dog can bring joy and friendship like none other. Keep this book handy and reference it often. Also, look for other resources, such as training books, get advices from experienced friends with dogs that can share their successes and failures. Never stop broadening your training skills. Your efforts will serve to keep you and your Australian Shepherd happy and healthy for a long, long time.

The Australian Shepherd is undoubtedly a very wise dog that possesses great qualities. In reality, they are highly acclaimed for being a smart working dog, very protective of their owner and family, has strong guarding and herding instincts, it is a breed that thinks life is limitless, it can manipulate its environment, and it is deemed as aggressive and authoritative. This breed is a must-have, for it is the type that loves its family beyond measure. It tolerates strangers with dignity but not enthusiastic affection.

I hope you find it useful throughout your life with your Australian Shepherd and keep it handy to refer back to when you have questions or concerns.

I also hope it inspires you to seek out more information on the amazing Australian Shepherd. No one resource can tell you everything you need to know, and I hope you keep learning more from other books and articles online and offline. I've made this a complete overview, but I hope you don't view this conclusion as the end of your learning journey.

Thank you for reading, and thank you for opening your heart to the Aussie and making every effort to be a great Aussie parent. I wish you and your Australian Shepherd many happy and healthy years together!

CPSIA information can be obtained
at www.ICGtesting.com
Printed in the USA
BVHW082330030521
606340BV00008B/2069